Sports

I Can Ice Skate

By Edana Eckart

Children's Press®
A Division of Scholastic Inc.
New York / Toronto / London / Auckland / Sydney
Mexico City / New Delhi / Hong Kong
Danbury, Connecticut

Photo Credits: Cover and all photos by Maura B. McConnell
Contributing Editor: Jennifer Silate
Book Design: Christopher Logan

Library of Congress Cataloging-in-Publication Data

Eckart, Edana.
    I can ice skate / by Edana Eckart.
        p. cm. — (Sports)
    Summary: When a young girl and her father go ice skating, she shows how
    to skate properly and safely.
    Includes bibliographical references and index.
    ISBN 0-516-23971-6 (lib. bdg.) — ISBN 0-516-24029-3 (pbk.)
    1. Skating—Juvenile literature. [1. Ice skating.] I. Title.

    GV848.95 .E35 2002
    796.91—dc21

                                                          2002001405

Contents

1 Ice Skates   6

2 The Rink   10

3 Time to Go   20

4 New Words   22

5 To Find Out More   23

6 Index   24

7 About the Author   24

My name is Millie.

Dad and I are going ice skating today.

5

I must wear special **skates** to ice skate.

Each skate has a long **blade** on the bottom.

7

I also wear warm clothes to ice skate.

My **gloves** will keep my hands warm.

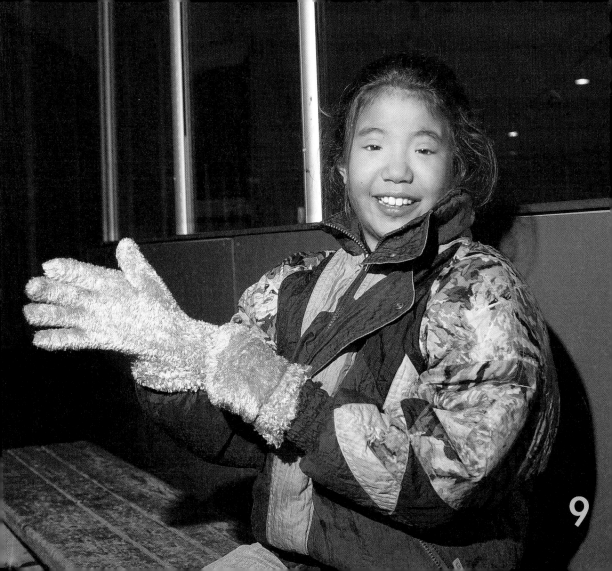

9

I will skate on a **rink**.

The rink is made of ice.

11

We are ready to ice skate.

I put one foot in front of the other.

I push off with my back foot.

I skate slowly.

I am careful not to fall.

14

15

It is time to turn.

I **lean** on my left leg.

I push with my right leg.

17

Dad and I skate around the rink.

Ice skating is fun!

19

It is time to go.

I take off my skates.

I cannot wait to go
ice skating again!

21

New Words

blade (**blayd**) the thin, metal strip on the bottom of an ice skate

gloves (**gluhvz**) warm hand coverings that have separate parts for each finger

lean (**leen**) to bend toward or over something

rink (**ringk**) an area with a specially prepared surface of ice that is used for ice skating

skates (**skayts**) boots with a blade on the bottom

To Find Out More

Books
Slip! Slide! Skate!
by Gail Herman
Scholastic Inc.

Sophie Skates
by Rachel Isadora
The Putnam Publishing Group

Web Site
Kid's Domain Ice Skating
http://www.kidsdomain.com/sports/iceskate/
Play ice skating games, print out pictures to color, or send e-cards to your friends on this fun Web site.

Index

blade, 6

clothes, 8

gloves, 8

ice, 10

rink, 10, 18

skate, 6, 20

About the Author
Edana Eckart has written several children's books. She enjoys bike riding with her family.

Reading Consultants
Kris Flynn, Coordinator, Small School District Literacy, The San Diego County Office of Education

Shelly Forys, Certified Reading Recovery Specialist, W.J. Zahnow Elementary School, Waterloo, IL

Sue McAdams, Former President of the North Texas Reading Council of the IRA, and Early Literacy Consultant, Dallas, TX